A World of Difference

Good Morning, Let's Eat!

By Karin Luisa Badt

CHILDRENS PRESS®
CHICAGO

Picture Acknowledgments

Cover (top left), NASA; cover (top right), © Mauritius/SuperStock International, Inc.; cover (center left), © AGE FotoStock/SuperStock International, Inc.; cover (bottom right), © Freeman/Grishaber/PhotoEdit; 1, SuperStock International, Inc.; 3 (left, © Mauritius/SuperStock International, Inc.; 3 (top right), © Robert W. Ginn/Unicorn Stock Photos; 3 (bottom right), © Buddy Mays/Travel Stock; 4 (top), © Robert Frerck/Odyssey/Frerck/Chicago; 4 (bottom), © Cameramann International, Ltd.; 5 (left), © Buddy Mays/Travel Stock; 5 (top right), © Robert Frerck/Odyssey/Frerck/Chicago; 5 (bottom right), UPI/Bettmann; 6 (top right), © Felicia Martinez/PhotoEdit; 6 (left), © Doug Adams/Unicorn Stock Photos; 6 (bottom right), © Jim Shippee/Unicorn Stock Photos; 7 (top), © Tony Freeman/PhotoEdit; 7 (center and bottom), © AGE FotoStock/SuperStock International, Inc.; 8 (top left), © Ernest Manewal/SuperStock International, Inc.; 8 (top right), © Cameramann International, Ltd.; 8 (bottom), © Jason Lauré/Valan; 9 (top), UPI/Bettmann Newsphotos; 9 (bottom), © Freeman/Grishaber/PhotoEdit; 10 (top), © AGE FotoStock/SuperStock International, Inc.; 10 (bottom), © John Elk III; 11 (top left), © Buddy Mays/Travel Stock; 11 (top right), © Robert Llewellyn/SuperStock International, Inc.; 11 (bottom), © G. Beery/Photri; 12, © Chip and Rosa Maria de la Cueva Peterson; 13 (top), Reuters/Bettmann; 13 (bottom), © T. Firak/Photri; 14 (left), © A. Gurmankin/Unicorn Stock Photos; 14 (top right), SuperStock International, Inc.; 14 (bottom right), © C. Osborne/Valan; 15 (top), © Cameramann International, Ltd.; 15 (bottom left), © Tony Freeman/PhotoEdit; 15 (bottom right), © Buddy Mays/Travel Stock; 16 (top), © Robert W. Ginn/Unicorn Stock Photos; 16 (bottom), © Brian Seed/Tony Stone Images; 17 (top), © John Elk III; 17 (bottom), UPI/Bettmann; 18 (left), © Cameramann International, Ltd.; 18 (top right), © John Eastcott/Yva Momatiuk/Valan; 18 (bottom right), © Wendy Stone/Odyssey/Chicago; 19 (top left), © Roy Luckow/Valan; 19 (top right), © Robert Frerck/Odyssey/Frerck/Chicago; 19 (bottom), © Christine Osborne/Valan; 20 (top), © Jean Higgins/Unicorn Stock Photos; 20 (center), © Kennon Cooke/Valan; 20 (bottom), © Christine Osborne/Valan; 21 (top left), © Charles E. Schmidt/Unicorn Stock Photos; 21 (right), © John Eastcott/Yva Momatiuk/Valan; 21 (bottom left), © Buddy Mays/Travel Stock; 22 (left), © Frank and Jauretta Carl/Unicorn Stock Photos; 22 (top right), © Clara Parsons/Valan; 22 (bottom right), © Val and Alan Wilkinson/Valan; 23, © Wendy Stone/Odyssey/Chicago; 24 (top), © Don Smetzer/Tony Stone Images; 24 (bottom), © John Eastcott/Yva Momatiuk/Valan; 25 (top), © Mike Boroff/Photri; 25 (center), © Steven Rothfeld/Tony Stone Images; 25 (bottom), © Steve Vidler/SuperStock International, Inc.; 26 (top), © Robert Brenner/PhotoEdit; 26 (bottom), © Don Smetzer/Tony Stone Images; 27 (top left), © Robert Frerck/Odyssey/Frerck/Chicago; 27 (top right), © K. Ghani/Valan; 27 (bottom), © C. Osborne/Valan; 28 (left), © Richard Nowitz/Valan; 28 (top right), © Robert Frerck/Odyssey/Frerck/Chicago; 28 (bottom right), © Rhoda Sidney/PhotoEdit; 29 (left), UPI/Bettmann; 29 (top right), © David Young-Wolff/PhotoEdit; 29 (bottom right), Reuters/Bettmann; 30 (top), © Val and Alan Wilkinson/Valan; 30 (bottom left), © Buddy Mays/Travel Stock; 30 (bottom right), © Robert Frerck/Odyssey/Frerck/Chicago; 31 (top), © Buddy Mays/Travel Stock; 31 (bottom left), © David Young-Wolff/PhotoEdit; 31 (bottom right), © Christine Osborne/Valan

On the cover

Top: Continental breakfast
Middle: Fried egg
Bottom: Vietnamese boy eating rice

On the title page

French *croissant*

Project Editor Shari Joffe
Design Beth Herman Design Associates
Photo Research Feldman & Associates

The author would like to thank Marshall Sahlins, Andy Apter, Raymond Fogelson, William Balan-Gaubert, Eric Budd, and David Graeber for their valuable input.

Badt, Karin Luisa.
   Good morning, let's eat! / by Karin Luisa Badt.
      p. cm. — (A world of difference)
   Includes index.
   ISBN 0-516-08190-X
      1. Food habits — Juvenile literature. 2. Breakfast — Juvenile literature. [1. Food habits. 2. Breakfast.] I. Title. II. Series.
   GT2850.B33 1994
   391.1`2 — dc20   94-12645
                                                                    CIP
                                                                    AC

Contents

What is This Thing Called Breakfast?

Right now, somewhere in the world, the sun is rising. People are getting ready for a new day. For most people, that includes eating breakfast. Where does this name for the day's first meal come from? *Fast* means "a time of not eating." When we *break* our *fast,* we put an end to it—in other words, we eat! After hours of going without food while we sleep, we are naturally a little hungry when we wake up. A good breakfast satisfies our hunger and gives us the energy we need to start the day.

What is a good breakfast? Pancakes and sausage? Beans and rice? Eggs and bananas? Nutritionists— people who know what food contains and how it affects the body—have some pretty definite ideas. Many people try to follow those ideas in order to stay healthy. But custom also plays a big part in determining what we eat for breakfast. We tend to eat what our families taught us to eat. And families in different cultures have very different ideas about what is good to eat in the morning.

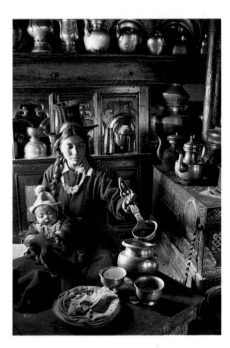

Ladakh, India

In most countries around the world, people eat some type of morning meal. *What* people eat for breakfast, however, varies widely from culture to culture.

Malaysia These men are enjoying a traditional Malaysian breakfast at a village cafe.

Mexico City, Mexico

South Africa
This Zulu woman is preparing a traditional breakfast of corn or wheat mush over a fire.

United States
Breakfast gives people the energy they need to start the day!

What Makes Breakfast Different from Other Meals?

In many cultures, breakfast is not only the first meal of the day—it is *different* from the other meals of the day. Certain foods are eaten only for breakfast, while others are eaten only for lunch or dinner. For example, in parts of Europe and the United States, pancakes and waffles are breakfast foods. They generally aren't eaten at other meals. The Ashanti people of Ghana have a dish eaten only at breakfast called *kontomire ne momone*. It is made by mashing taro-plant leaves together with salted fish, tomatoes, and onions, and then drizzling turmeric-spiced palm oil on top.

Packaged cereal In North America, packaged cereals—made from such grains as wheat, corn, rice, rye, or oats—are extremely popular for breakfast. Packaged cereals were invented in the United States in the 1800s.

Waffles and pancakes In the United States, waffles and pancakes are considered breakfast foods. They are not likely to be eaten at other times of day.

Danish round pancakes In Denmark, pancakes are not eaten for breakfast, but as a special treat that might be served after lunch or dinner. The Netherlands is another place where pancakes are not considered breakfast food. Dutch pancakes, called *pannekoeken*, are made with a variety of fillings—such as cheese, vegetables, or apples and brown sugar—and are served as a main course for lunch or dinner.

Of course, a food that one culture considers "breakfast food" may be "dinner food" in another culture. For example, the British often eat fried eggs for breakfast. In their culture, eggs are a breakfast food. Italians, however, do not eat eggs for breakfast. For them, eggs are a food you eat for dinner. They may be served sunny-side up (fried on one side only) or made into a *frittata* (a kind of omelette) with parsley and green onions.

French omelette Omelettes—usually eaten for breakfast in the United States—are eaten only for lunch or dinner in France.

Eggs Eggs are popular for breakfast in many countries. The British often eat them fried for breakfast.

7

Woman preparing breakfast, Russia In Russia, breakfast differs from other meals in that it is the biggest meal of the day. The *kinds* of foods eaten at breakfast, however, often don't differ from those eaten at other meals.

Papua New Guinea Sago, a staple food of Papua New Guinea, may be a part of any meal, including breakfast. It is prepared by scooping out the starchy pith from the inside of the sago palm tree and grating it into flour. After the flour is mixed with water, it is eaten as a mush or pudding, or baked into flat bread.

Not all cultures have special "breakfast foods." The native people of Fiji eat their staple foods—taro and yams—for breakfast, lunch, and dinner. The Durrani people of Afghanistan eat three meals a day. The first two meals are the same: *dodey* (bread), tea, and milk or cheese. In the evening, the Durrani usually eat a hot meal of stew, soup, rice pudding, and *dodey*.

San women gathering edible roots, Botswana In some hunter-gatherer societies, the people do not eat meals at specific times of day, but at times when they find food. Traditionally, the San people of the Kalahari Desert were hunter-gatherers. Today, however, few San follow their traditional pattern of hunting and gathering. Most earn a living by working for other Africans as cattle herders or on cattle ranches.

Israel In Israel, the traditional breakfast is the same as the traditional dinner: cheese, tomatoes, cucumbers, salad, yogurt, pickles, and boiled eggs.

Vietnam Staple foods are the ones that provide the bulk of a nation's everyday diet. In most East Asian countries, rice is a staple food that is eaten with every meal, including breakfast.

Moreover, not everyone in the world divides up their meals into "breakfast," "lunch," and "dinner." Some, like the Sirionó Indians of Bolivia, eat whenever they have food, which may be at different times each day. In some cultures, people eat many tiny meals throughout the day, starting with a tidbit for breakfast. The Jorai of Southeast Asia, for example, eat all day long, snacking on fruits, insects, and birds in the forests. Their "breakfast" consists of the first snack they happen to find.

Big and Small Breakfasts

In some cultures, a traditional breakfast is small and light, while in others, it is a substantial meal. A typical Portuguese breakfast is merely a cup of coffee with a sweet pastry. In Norway, on the other hand, big breakfasts are the rule. Norwegians like to eat cold fish, meat, and cheese, with big chunks of bread or crispy wafers for breakfast. Russia is another place where big breakfasts are popular. There, a typical breakfast consists of several types of cheese, meat, fish, and salad.

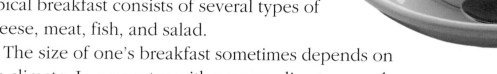

The size of one's breakfast sometimes depends on the climate. In a country with a warm climate, people

Dutch breakfast Large, filling breakfasts that may include eggs, cheeses, breads, and cold meats or fish have traditionally been popular in such northern European countries as The Netherlands, Germany, Norway, Denmark, Sweden, and Finland.

Kazakhstan A large communal breakfast of lamb and bread is traditional for the people of Kazakhstan.

may not feel like beginning the day with a huge, heavy meal. A big breakfast combined with the hot sun may make them feel drowsy. But in a cold country, it can be nice to wake up to a hearty breakfast. When it's cold outside, you burn more energy, and therefore need more food to get through the day.

Portuguese pastries Typically, people eat light breakfasts in Portugal; perhaps a cup of coffee with one of Portugal's many kinds of sweet pastries.

American breakfast Traditionally, the United States has been known for its big breakfasts.

Breakfast size may also vary according to the size of the other meals of the day. In many cultures around the world, the noon or afternoon meal is the most important one. Children come home from school and adults come home from work to sit together and enjoy a big meal. In these cultures, breakfast is usually very small. Otherwise, no one would have an appetite for such a large lunch! In Iran, for example, people usually have a light breakfast of bread and cheese. At lunchtime, Iranians get together for a very filling meal of rice, meat, and vegetables. In Spain, the big meal of the day is served mid-afternoon. Breakfast typically consists only of *pan con mantequilla*—bread with butter.

In China, the evening dinner is the most important meal. The Chinese usually eat a medium-sized breakfast of rice with vegetables. In southeastern China, people may instead eat *zi* (dumplings), *you tiao* (fried dough), or *da bin* (salty sesame cakes) for breakfast.

Continental breakfast, Switzerland A light, "continental" breakfast—bread, rolls, or pastries served with coffee or tea—has traditionally been popular in such central and southern European countries as France, Switzerland, Italy, Portugal, and Spain. Continental breakfasts are also popular in many South American countries. Can you think of a reason why big breakfasts are more common in northern countries, while small breakfasts are more popular in the south?

Chinese family making dumplings Chinese breakfasts, which are usually medium-sized, may include various kinds of dumplings.

***Pan con mantequilla,* Spain** In Spain, people usually eat four meals a day. *El desayuno* is a small continental breakfast of bread with butter. At around 11:00 A.M., it is time for *el bocata*—another small meal. This might be a thick piece of omelette. The big meal of the day—*la comida*—is served around 2:30 P.M. Everyone comes home and spends up to two hours eating a variety of foods. They do not eat again until 10:00 or 11:00 P.M., when they have *la cena*—a small supper.

Sweet or Salty?

Around the world, people have very different ideas about what tastes good for breakfast. In some cultures, people like to have a sweet breakfast. The French, for example, often eat sweet, buttery pastries called *croissants.* People in Scotland eat hot scones—a type of biscuit— with jam or honey.

And in Switzerland, people often wake up to toast and marmalade.

In other cultures, it is the custom to eat salty or tangy foods at breakfast time. In Egypt and other countries in the Middle East, a typical breakfast dish is *foul mudammas:* fava beans mixed with olive oil and lemon juice. Many Arabs in the Middle East also like thick slices of feta, a salty white cheese. The Yoruba of Nigeria usually eat beans and rice or a fried bean cake called *akara* for breakfast. They would never eat a sweet breakfast. They believe that eating sugar—at any time of the day—is unhealthy.

The Japanese typically prepare a dish of rice with *nori* (a kind of seaweed) for breakfast. They also have a traditional breakfast soup called *misoshiru.* It is made

Scottish scone

French *croissant* In France, sweet, crescent-shaped flaky rolls called *croissants* are often eaten with butter and jam for breakfast.

Cheese seller, Syria In countries in the Middle East, people often eat pieces of *feta,* a salty white cheese, as part of their breakfast.

Japanese breakfast A typical Japanese breakfast includes such salty foods as *miso* soup, *nori* (seaweed), grilled fish, pickled vegetables, and salad.

of rice, tofu, vegetables, nori, and *miso*—a salty paste made of fermented soybeans. Sometimes they warm up this soup later in the day and eat it for lunch or dinner as well.

In the Czech Republic, a traditional breakfast consists of sliced peppers, meat, and cheese, along with buttered pieces of bread. Sometimes the Czechs even eat hot dogs for breakfast!

Boy selling sweet breakfast rolls, Mexico

German sausages In some countries, sweet foods are combined with salty foods for breakfast. For example, in Germany, a traditional breakfast consists of cold cuts, *wurst* (sausage), *brotchen* (rolls), and bread and marmalade.

In Hungary, people sometimes eat a chocolate pastry called *kakoas csicta* along with toast, eggs, salami, and buttered bread.

In many countries, breakfast is different depending on whether you live in an urban area or a rural area. City people usually buy their food in stores. They are able to buy foods from other countries—American cereal, French cheese, or Hungarian sausage—or from other parts of their own country.

In rural areas, people are more likely to produce at least some of their own food.

For example, people in rural areas of Lebanon usually make their own feta for breakfast. They wash down this salty cheese with plenty of milk from their own goats and cows!

Woman baking her own bread, Ireland

Woman winnowing rice, Malaysia In most countries, rural people are more likely than urban people to produce at least some of their own food for breakfast.

Woman sorting maize (corn), Zaire

Family making bean curd, China

Woman grinding grain, India

Shopping at a supermarket, The Gambia Urban people usually buy their breakfast food in stores. This gives them access to foods from other countries, as well as foods from other parts of their own country.

City people may eat a different breakfast than do rural people because of the kind of work they do. Many people in urban and suburban areas have to be at work early in the morning—and may have a long commute. They may not have time to sit down and eat a big breakfast. Instead, they may "grab a bite" on the way to work. For example, in Turkish cities, people on the way to work may buy a *borek*—a spicy pastry filled with cheese, meat, and vegetables—from one of the many vendors who sell breakfast food along the street.

Seattle

Athens, Greece

Breakfast on the go City people sometimes don't have time to eat a big breakfast. Instead, they may "grab a bite" on the way to work.

Banjul, The Gambia

Hearty rural breakfast, Scotland In many countries, farmers typically wake up early and sit down to a large breakfast before tackling the morning's chores.

Farmers, on the other hand, do not have to rush to work. They typically wake up very early and take the time to enjoy a substantial meal. That way, they have the energy they need for the morning's tasks, which are often physically demanding.

Farm girl doing morning chores, Canada

Dairy farmer and cows in the Dorset Hills, England

Often, wealthy people and poor people in the same country eat different breakfasts. For example, in the Philippines, a typical breakfast for wealthy people is rice, dried fish, eggs, sausage, and juice. Poorer people also eat rice and dried fish, but not eggs, sausage, or juice, because they can't afford them.

Vendor selling dried-fish, Philippines In the Philippines, dried fish is a breakfast food eaten by rich and poor alike.

Vendor selling white bread, Nigeria In many parts of Africa, however, white bread is still prestigious. Most of Africa was once under European rule. Perhaps wealthy native Africans prefer white bread, even though it has less nutritional value, because it was eaten by the people who once had power over them.

White bread and whole-wheat bread
For hundreds of years, most people in Europe ate dark, whole-grain bread. White bread was too expensive because it was more difficult to make. As long as only rich people could afford it, white bread had higher prestige than dark bread. Then, in the late 1800s, millers developed machinery to make white flour inexpensively, and white bread became the most popular kind. But a funny thing happened: people discovered that whole-grain bread is healthier then white bread. Because many people are now more health-conscious than they used to be, whole-grain bread is now often more prestigious—and more costly!

In Nigeria, wealthy Yoruba people who live in the cities do not eat the traditional *akara*. They like to eat a Western-type breakfast of cornflakes, eggs, and bleached white bread. These foods may not taste any better than bean cakes, but they cost more and thus have higher prestige. In Haiti, rich people typically eat eggs, toast, marmalade, warm milk, and bananas for breakfast. Poorer people in Haiti may have a slice of *bobotte*—a heavy bread—and herring for breakfast.

Rural market, Papua New Guinea In most developing countries, many of the people are poor. Because they cannot afford to buy enough food or a wide variety of foods, many suffer from an inadequate diet. Their breakfast—in fact, their diet in general—is limited to foods they can produce themselves: mainly grains or starchy root vegetables. Such foods are filling, inexpensive to produce, and require no refrigeration, but they do not provide all the nutrients people need to stay healthy. In Papua New Guinea, most people rely heavily on such starchy foods as sweet potatoes, yams, taro, sago, and bananas. Only some people can afford a more varied diet that includes such protein-rich foods such as meat or fish.

Breakfast is Served!

How people eat breakfast is just as interesting as *what* they eat. In the United States, people tend to eat breakfast while sitting down at a table, either alone or with others. In Senegal, people sit together on the ground and take their breakfast food from a communal bowl that is set in the middle. In Italy, people often eat breakfast standing up! Each morning, little coffee shops are filled with Italians standing at the counter, drinking their coffee and eating their *cornettos*.

In some cultures, it is customary to talk to other people while you eat. In other cultures, this is considered rude. For example, it is the tradition

Japan In Japan, people tend to eat breakfast while sitting down at a table, either alone or with others.

Inuit family, Canada In some cultures, people sit on the floor while eating breakfast and other meals. This Inuit family is eating a breakfast of freshly made *bannock* (a fried bread that is an Inuit staple) while sitting together on the floor of their tent.

Friends having breakfast together at a local coffee shop
In the United States, people sometimes read the newspaper while eating breakfast. Can you think of why it might be considered more acceptable to read at the breakfast table than at other meals?

in many American Indian tribes to eat alone. One does not bother others while they are eating.

Some cultures have customs about the order in which people eat. The people who have the highest status—perhaps because of age, gender, or wealth—help themselves or are served first. In Saudi Arabia, for example, men get to eat breakfast first, while women and children have to wait to eat whatever is left. In many cultures, guests are considered the most important people at the table, and so are served first.

Italy In Italy, people often eat breakfast standing at the counter of a neighborhood *caffé* (coffee shop).

China In China, families often sit together around a table and take their breakfast from communal bowls set in the middle.

The utensils that people use for breakfast also vary from culture to culture. In many places, especially Europe and North America, people use forks, knives, and spoons. The fork came into popular use in Europe about five hundred years ago. Before that, Europeans ate with their hands, though they did use knives for cutting the food into pieces. In parts of Asia, people use chopsticks for solid foods and spoons for soup. The people of Pohnpei, an island in the Federated States of Micronesia, have quite an unusual utensil for scooping up food: banana leaves!

Forks, knives, and spoons In many parts of the world, including Europe and North America, forks, knives, and spoons are the utensils people use while eating breakfast.

Chopsticks In East Asian countries such as China, Japan, Korea, and Vietnam, breakfast—like all other meals—is eaten with chopsticks. Knives are not needed with the cuisine of these countries because the food is cut into small pieces before being served. Chopsticks were first used in China around the 4th century B.C., and later spread to other countries of East Asia. In Chinese, chopsticks are called *k'uai-tzu*, which mean "quick ones."

Women making *chapatis*, India

Men having breakfast, India
In Pakistan and India, pieces of a flat bread called *chapati* are often used to scoop up food at breakfast and other meals.

In many places, people don't use utensils at all. Instead, they use bread to scoop up food: *pita* in southern Europe and the Middle East, *tortillas* in Mexico and Central America, *chapatis* and *pooris* in India, and many kinds of spongy bread in Africa. After the food is gone, the bread gets eaten too!

Woman drying maize that will be used make *injera*, Ethiopia
Injera is a spongy, slightly sour-tasting flat bread that Ethiopians use to scoop up food.

27

Something to Drink with Your Breakfast?

Girl eating *churros* and chocolate, Spain

What do people drink with their breakfast? In some cultures, nothing. For example, the Yao, who live in Thailand, Vietnam, and southern China, never drink during any meal.

In other cultures, the beverage is an important part of breakfast—sometimes even more important than the food. For example, many people feel that breakfast isn't breakfast without a cup of tea or coffee. Tea is a traditional Asian beverage. Trade made it possible for tea to become popular in Europe, Africa, the Americas, and the Middle East as well. Coffee is believed to have been invented in what is now Yemen, an Arab country, about a thousand years ago. By the fifteenth century, coffee was a common drink all over the Middle East. Eventually, through trade, it too became one of the most popular breakfast drinks in the world.

***Maté*, Argentina**
Maté is a tea-like drink popular for breakfast in Argentina. It is made from the dried leaves of the yerba maté tree, and is served in cups with cream and sugar.

The Yoruba typically drink a hot corn gruel (thin porridge) called *ekkaw* in the mornings—or sometimes

Bedouin man grinding coffee beans, Israel Coffee is enjoyed for breakfast in many parts of the world. It can be prepared either weak or strong. Turkish coffee is so thick that after you drink it, the empty cup looks muddy. By contrast, American coffee is often weak—almost like flavored hot water. In different parts of the world, people add different things to their coffee: milk, cream, sugar, or sometimes spices. People in Saudi Arabia and Kuwait, for example, put cardamom, a bitter herb, in their coffee.

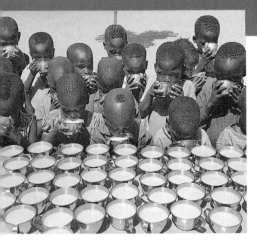

Schoolchildren drinking milk, Chad In many parts of the world, children start their day with a glass of milk. Milk is an excellent source of protein, which children need to help them grow. Few children in developing countries, however, are lucky enough to have milk. Here, children in Chad enjoy a morning cup of milk as part of a school nutritional supplement program.

Fruit juice Fruit juices are often a part of breakfast in warm countries where tropical fruits are grown. In the United States, orange juice is the most popular breakfast juice.

a cup of strong palm wine. In Spain, hot chocolate is often preferred over coffee, especially on Sundays, when people like to dip *churros* (fried strips of sweet dough) into it. In Switzerland, as in many other countries, a glass of milk is considered a nourishing and delicious way to begin the day.

Man pouring a cup of tea, England Tea is one of the world's most popular breakfast drinks. Tea was invented in China around 350 B.C., and made its way to Europe in the 1600s. Today, India, China, and Sri Lanka are the largest producers of tea. Great Britain imports the greatest amount of tea— about 400 million pounds per year. An average of 7 pounds of tea are consumed per person each year in Great Britain!

The World at Your Breakfast Table

raditionally, people have eaten breakfast foods that grow naturally or can be raised easily in their area. For example, the Japanese eat seaweed because they can get it easily from the sea. In Kenya, breakfast porridge is made with cassava because cassava grows naturally there. In Madagascar, an island country of Africa, rice grows well because of the warm, wet climate. Breakfast there is usually *vary amin'ny ananas:* rice with vegetables. In Guatemala, the traditional breakfast is corn tortillas topped with refried beans and sour cream. Corn and beans grow well in that Central American country.

Cassava plants, Cameroon
In many African countries, including Kenya, Nigeria, and Cameroon, breakfast porridge is made from cassava (a root vegetable) because cassava grows naturally there.

But people are not limited to eating foods that they can grow or find nearby. Ever since the beginning of civilization, people from different cultures have swapped both foods and ideas about how to prepare them.

Vendor selling corn at a local market, Ecuador (far left)

Woman making tortillas, Guatemala In Central and South American countries, where corn is a staple crop, corn pancakes called *tortillas* are commonly served at breakfast time.

Rice worker, Bali, Indonesia In Indonesia—as in many other East Asian countries—breakfast always includes rice. This is because rice thrives in the warm, wet climate of Indonesia.

Muesli *Muesli* (below left), a Swiss breakfast cereal made of rolled oats, nuts, and fruit, has become increasingly popular in North America.

The potato, for example, originally grew only in South America. Today, the potato is an important part of many breakfasts around the world. It's been turned into hash browns, potato pancakes, and potato knishes —just to name a few!

With the development of modern transportation, foods are being exchanged faster than ever. Breakfast is truly an international affair! In the United States, for example, breakfast can be eggs with refried beans (Costa Rican), pancakes (Scandinavian), croissants (French), or any of the innumerable foreign dishes that have become part of American culture. On the other hand, in places like Iran, American packaged cereals, like cornflakes, have become popular breakfast foods, especially among children.

With all the breakfasts in the world, we have many wonderful choices about how to begin our day!

Egyptian advertisement for American cereals

Glossary

appetite a desire for food or drink (p.12)

beverage a drink (p.28)

climate the average weather conditions of a place or region over a period of years (p.10)

communal referring to an activity done with a group of people (p.11)

culture the beliefs and customs of a group of people that are passed from one generation to another (p.4)

customary the way something is commonly done (p.24)

dumpling a small mass of dough cooked by boiling or steaming (p.12)

ethnic group a group of people whose members share the same culture, language, or customs (p.17)

immigrants people who come to a country or region where they were not born (p.17)

inadequate less than is needed; not adequate (p.23)

international relating to or affecting two or more nations (p.31)

marmalade a type of jam, usually made of citrus fruits (p.14)

nourishing referring to foods that provide what people need to keep alive and healthy (p.29)

nutrients the substances in foods that are nourishing (p.23)

nutritional nourishing (p.22)

pith the soft, spongy tissue that fills the center of the stems of certain plants (p.8)

prestigious given great value or importance (p.22)

protein a nutrient that is a necessary part of the human diet; it is found especially in meat, milk, nuts, and eggs (p.23)

rural of or relating to the country (p.18)

staple foods foods that provide the bulk of a nation's everyday diet (p.8)

starch a vegetable substance produced by many plants (p.8)

substantial large in amount (p.10)

taro a tropical plant that has an edible, starchy root (p.6)

traditional handed down from generation to generation (p.4)

turmeric an herb of the ginger family (p.6)

urban of or relating to the city (p.18)

winnow to sift out (p.18)

Index

About the Author

Karin Luisa Badt has a Ph.D. in comparative literature from the University of Chicago and a B.A. in literature and society from Brown University. She likes to travel and live in foreign countries. Ms. Badt has taught at the University of Rome and the University of Chicago.